MW01193774

Drills for Grapplers

*Training Drills And Games You Can Do On The Mat For
Jujitsu, Judo And Submission Grappling*

Drills for Grapplers

Training Drills And Games You Can Do On The Mat For Jujitsu, Judo And Submission Grappling

By Steve Scott

 Turtle Press   Santa Fe

Photos by Steve Scott, Mark Lozano and Jorge Garcia.

Cover Photo by Jorge Garcia.

To contact the author or to order additional copies of this book:
call 1-800-778-8785 or visit www.TurtlePress.com

ISBN 978-1-934903-04-9
LCCN 2008016036
Printed in the United States of America

10 9 8 7 6 5 4 3 2 1 0

Warning-Disclaimer

This book is designed to provide information on specific skills used in judo, jujitsu, sambo, grappling and other martial arts. It is not the purpose of this book to reprint all the information that is otherwise available to the author, publisher, printer or distributors, but instead to compliment, amplify and supplement other texts. You are urged to read all available material, learn as much as you wish about the subjects covered in this book and tailor the information to your individual needs. Anyone practicing the skills presented in this book should be physically capable to do so and have the permission of a licensed physician before participating in this activity or any physical activity.

Every effort has been made to make this book as complete and accurate as possible. However, there may be mistakes, both typographical and in content. Therefore, this text should be used only as a general guide and not the ultimate source of information on the subjects presented here in this book on sambo or any skill or subject. The purpose of this book is to provide information and entertain. The author, publisher, printer and distributors shall neither have liability nor responsibility to any person or entity with respect to loss or damages caused, or alleged to have been caused, directly or indirectly, by the information contained in this book.

Library of Congress Cataloguing in Publication Data

Scott, Steve, 1952-
 Drills for grapplers : training drills and games you can do on the mat for jujitsu, judo and submission grappling / by Steve Scott.
    p. cm.
Includes bibliographical references and index.
ISBN 978-1-934903-04-9 (alk. paper)
1. Hand-to-hand fighting. 2. Self-defense. 3. Martial arts--Training. I. Title.
GV1112.S452 2008
796.81--dc22
                                    2008016036

Contents

INTRODUCTION

This book is about training effectively with special emphasis on drill training. It's for anyone in any form of sport combat or grappling, whether you do judo, jujitsu, sambo, submission grappling, mixed martial arts or any other form of martial art. The premise of this book presents two primary, core beliefs. They're pretty straightforward: 1-Train Hard and 2-Train Smart. This book is based on my earlier book COACHING ON THE MAT that was aimed primarily at coaches but useful for athletes as well. This book is directed primarily at athletes but will be useful for coaches who want some ideas on training and, more specifically, drill training.

Unless you are a professional and someone is paying you to train full-time, you have limited, and precious, time to devote to your training. You need to get the most out of your training every time and you need to train in the most efficient manner possible. The drills in this book may or may not be completely new to you, but they are tried and true and have been used by many champions. A common theme in all my books is that any information presented is realistic in both concept and execution. The drills shown in this book have produced winning results for many years.

The purpose of this book is to offer advice on effective training and how (and why) drill training are so important if you want to succeed in any form of sport combat or self-defense. This book is directed at showing you specific drills and games that can be done on the mat or in the training room and won't concern itself with some subjects such as periodization, training off the mat in the weight room, gym or outdoors for cardio and strength development. The primary focus of this book will be on showing you how you can use drills, games and on-the-mat training exercises to get more out of you training while on the mat.

Many thanks go to the members of the Welcome Mat Judo and Jujitsu Club who helped so much in the photo shoots and writing of this book. My wife Becky, who as an athlete, endured the drills presented in this book, was instrumental in offering advice and direction to me as I wrote it and I thank her for it. Special thanks also go to Cynthia Kim and Turtle Press for the professional advice and support offered in the production of this book. I also want to thank John Saylor, Bob Corwin and Jim Schneweis for their input, ideas and support. John Saylor is an innovative coach who used drill training very effectively with elite athletes when he was the coach at the U.S.

Olympic Training Center in Colorado Springs, Colorado and continues to use drill training at his Barn of Truth in Perrysville, Ohio where he trains athletes in Shingitai Jujitsu and MMA. Bob Corwin has used many of the drills presented in this book, plus many of his own unique drills and games, at his Yorkville, Illinois Judo Club for many years producing hundreds of national and international champions. Jim Schneweis is one of the best teachers and coaches I have ever worked with and has taken many kids off the street and turned them into wrestling champions at Ward High School in Kansas City, Kansas. I have fond memories of many hours on the mat with these great coaches, exchanging ideas and working on new drills. I also want to thank Pat Burris for urging me to write this book. Pat's a good friend and one of the best judo athletes and coaches to ever come from the United States. He was a member of two U.S. Olympic judo teams and served as the head coach for the U.S. Olympic Team as well. I appreciate his friendship, support and advice. These men are some of the best coaches I have ever worked with and their advice during the writing of this book is appreciated very much. Finally, I want to fondly mention Rene Pommerelle who, while he was alive and active as a coach, touched many judo athletes, including me, and taught me the importance of effective drill training. Some of Rene's drills and drill training concepts are presented in this book.

HOW TO USE THIS BOOK

Drill training is structured learning and structured training. A good drill helps you improve and a good drill is one that is practical. A drill should relate to something that is important to you, whether it is improved fitness, learning how to perform a new skill better or how to get a tactical advantage over an opponent. If a drill isn't practical, it's pretty much useless and nothing more than going through the motions.

This book doesn't contain all the drills or training games ever invented. However, the information presented in this book has been proven effective by many athletes and on many mats and I hope you can use this book as a reliable training and coaching resource for many years to come. Take the information in this book and make it work for you. Don't hesitate to make a change in a drill or game to make it fit your needs. By the way, most of the drills and games in this book can be done with or without a training jacket. If you're a grappler who doesn't wear a jujitsu or judogi, you can adapt these drills to fit your needs.

In this book, you'll see terms like "randori," "uchikomi," and other Japanese words. Many of you reading this come from a judo or jujitsu background, but many others don't. I'm not trying to exclude anyone, but the Japanese terms used in this book really do a good job in describing the purpose, action or reason for a drill. For this reason, I'll use the Japanese word from time to time, but will always explain it as thoroughly as possible. I sincerely believe a good skill is a good skill no matter what you call it or who taught it to you. It just so happens in some cases, the Japanese phrase is more descriptive and when this happens, it will be used.

Honestly, the use of effective drills in your training will make a huge difference in your skill, fitness level and the results that come from improved skill and fitness. It's hoped that the information in this book will help you achieve your goals.

SECTION ONE:
Training Concepts

"Success is an on-going process."
Steve Scott

THE IMPORTANCE OF DRILL TRAINING

Years ago, I got to know Mel Bruno, one of America's judo pioneers and a leading coach of his era. Mel had an extensive background in both judo and wrestling and he gave me some of the best advice I ever heard. I was a young athlete and coach in judo and sambo at the time and Mel and I were discussing the most effective ways of training judo athletes. He said; "Teach them judo, but train them like wrestlers." What he meant was that you should not only train with intensity, but also train with purpose. Mel's advice was that I should teach good, skillful judo and use the performance-based methods of training that are used so effectively in wrestling. Every training session, practice or workout must include effective drill training along with an effective level of randori (going live or practice matches) training. Use your time wisely as an athlete and a coach and don't waste any precious training time while on the mat. You have only a limited, specific amount of time each day or week when you are on the mat, so use it wisely. Train hard, but also train smart. Mel told me that as a wrestling coach (and as a judo coach) he included plenty of drill training time for his athletes and this made the difference between the "tough guys" and the champions. Since that time, I've tried to follow Mel's advice and I'm glad I did.

Drill training is used to develop skills in any situation where learning takes place. In a grappling sense, drill training is used to teach and reinforce skill, fitness, confidence, aerobic fitness, anaerobic fitness, overall strategy and specific tactics. Drill training is a useful psychological tool for a coach as it instills a desire on the athlete's part to continually improve.

Drill Training is Concentrated Learning

Drill training is what I call "concentrated learning." What I mean is that drill training takes a specific action, movement or situation and focuses in on it entirely. If you want to develop a specific skill, you can use a drill to work on it. Drill training is the controlled repetition of any movement and the athlete can use it to reinforce a pattern of behavior or movement to improve his performance in that specific skill, technique, tactic or physical situation (such as strength or cardio training).

Drill training eliminates, to a great extent, the goofing off that can take place in a practice session. Through intelligent drill training, the athlete can learn skills more easily and the coach can regulate time better, avoiding boredom in practice. Drills can prevent a team from going stale because drill training provides a variety of situations in training.

Really, just about any situation in any sport or self-defense can be drilled on and should be, for that matter. Drills can be used to teach new skills and maintain and reinforce already-learned techniques. A drill can be designed for about every facet or grappling movement or action and reaction. Drills can be done either static (where the partners don't move a great deal such as in "static" uchikomi or repetition training) or can be done in moving situations.

There are two major types of drills that will be discussed in this book:

1. Fitness Drills

These drills and games are used to improve cardio fitness, strength, flexibility, coordination, agility or other physical attributes. They also can be used to toughen up athletes and get them used to the rigors of hard training and hard fighting. For this reason, fitness drills are useful for both physical and psychological improvement.

2. Skill Drills

These drills emphasize the teaching or reinforcing of skill, technique, strategy and tactics. Athletes work on specific skills or moves with varying degrees of cooperation so that an instinctive behavior in a skill or specific technique is accomplished. With this in mind, there are 2 types of Skill Drills:

A. Closed-ended Drills:

These teach or reinforce specific behavior. This is also called a "fixed drill" and the athlete must work on a specific skill, game or exercise repeatedly to develop that skill into an instinctive reaction. A good example of this type of drill is Uchikomi (Repetition or Fit-in Drills) where an athlete performs many repetitions of a specific skill or technique and gets the benefit of developing that technique so that it is second nature to him.

B. Open-ended Drills:

These are drills where the athlete is often presented with a basic or specific situation and he must adapt or react to it using his own methods or already-learned skills or tactics. A classic example of this type of drill is randori, or free practice, which is a fighting drill, and will be discussed in the next paragraph. But, there is a specific variation of Open-ended Drills that are situation or fighting drills and this leads to the following:

B1. Situational Drills or Fighting Drills.

These drills emphasize learning, reacting to and developing what to do in a specific situation using "real world" skills, movement and behavior. You can develop realistic drills by carefully observing situations that come up in actual matches or situations (or self-defense situations). A good example of a Situational Drill is to place an athlete in a specific situation and make him fight out of it. In MMA training for example, the coach can put an athlete up against the cage (or in a corner if they are training for a fight in a boxing ring) and have his training partner place him in a specific situation. His job is to fight out of that predicament. The coach can have the training partner offer varying degrees of resistance and realism and the coach should emphasize the correct tactics or skills to use in that situation. Another example of a Situational Drill is to place one grappler in his opponent's guard and the job of the bottom grappler (the one in the guard position) is to keep the top grappler from getting out. The athletes can go varying levels of resistance and the coach should make it a point to coach the athletes on the correct technical skills and tactics to use when in this situation.

Often, the value of drills will overlap so that a drill that is primarily a skill drill will often have value as a fitness drill or situational drill. When listing the various drills and games in this book, I placed the drill in the section where it's primary function is, but remember, drill training is very real and very physical, so most every drill has benefits in all areas of development.

Drills can be performed in ideal situations or realistic situations. A coach can use a drill to teach instinctive behavior with both athletes cooperating 100% with each other. I often use this type of "Skill Drill" in training athletes. A good example is the "Spinning Juji Drill" where the athletes work on their Juji Gatame (Cross-body Armlock). One partner does the spinning application of the cross-body armlock and his partner offers no resistance. The athletes either do this is sets of 3 repetitions each for a set amount of time or I time one athlete and he does as many good repetitions as possible in the time allotted. What this does is reinforce an effective skill and teaches the athlete performing it to do it instinctively. The old saying "Good practice produces good results" is true. Doing a skill correctly over and over again reinforces it and makes it an instinctive behavior.

Drills can be changed so that one athlete offers 100% cooperation or 100% resistance. I recommend that coaches vary the cooperation levels when conducting drill training to accurately copy what may actually take place in a real situation.

Drill Training is Efficient

Drill training is necessary for improvement in athletic performance. It creates a disciplined, stable training atmosphere and is conducive to better learning and teamwork. Don't be fooled into thinking the only way you can make progress is to fight your training partners every time and in every practice. If all you do is show up, warm up, than "roll" for an hour, the odds that you will make any serious improvement are slim to none.

To develop any movement or technique to a high degree of skill and to make it fit you like a glove, it's important to have consistent, directed and mechanically correct practice. This is what drill training is: consistent, directed (aimed) at the development of that specific skill, and done in a way that is mechanically (technically) correct form for that specific skill. Drill training keys in on developing the move you want to make improvement on and gives you the opportunity to make that move or technique something you can (and will) do instinctively when you need to. In a match or actual self-defense situation, you must be able to perform the skill without having to take the time to think through it. It must be instinctive for it to work best for you. Also, drill training teaches you to be efficient in how you perform the skill you are training on. You learn, through repeated drill training, to perform the skill with maximum effect and expend minimum energy to do it. During the early stages of learning any skill, there is a good amount of body tension that is natural to all of us as human beings. You haven't trained your muscles to perform in the way you want them to in order to perform the skill. By learning the mechanically and fundamentally correct way of doing a movement, then practicing it correctly, both the body and mind adapt and you learn the skill or movement. But, if you randomly work on the movement or skill, your chances of doing it well (much less instinctively) are not very good. Drill training is the tool that enables efficient learning and performance to take place. For instance, if you want to improve your cross-body armlock and if you only fight every training session, you most likely will only be able to pull it off a few times during any given training session. If everybody in your club knows you want to work on it and all you do is fight each other, then it will be a rare training partner indeed who lets you catch him in it. On the other hand, if you take a good portion of your training time and devote it to drill training, you will be better able to work on your cross-body armlock (or any skill for that matter) and make the technique an instinctive behavior.

Don't get me wrong. You need time to go live, randori, roll, or have practice matches just about every training session, but don't make your entire training time just that. Drill training is training smart and training hard. Having a training session of just fighting each other is training hard, but not always training smart. When it comes down to two grapplers who are equal in how hard they train, the one who trains smarter will win. He's the one who has better skill. By the same token, if all you do is work on isolated technique training and don't emphasize randori or practice matches as part of your training, you need to include effective drill training to reinforce and improve skills and make them instinctive behavior. An example is training in a martial art that is not adapted to sport combat or grappling. The self-defense athletes who train in Krav Maga, Systema or other non-sport martial disciplines need drill training as much as competitive grapplers in judo, sambo, submission grappling, MMA and sport jujitsu. Many jujitsu systems don't look at their martial art as a sporting activity, but drill training is just as important to them as a competitive athlete.

When learning the fundamentals of any skill, or when the coach introduces a new skill or concept (even to elite athletes), the skill drills should be (at first) closed-ended so that the specific technique can be correctly learned.

This means that the athletes performing the drill should cooperate so that maximum learning and performance take place. However, the drill training should be as realistic as possible, so the coach should make sure that what is being taught and drilled on is effective, realistic and mechanically correct. Coaches, I want to tell you that drill training isn't a time when you instruct or coach your athletes. Include time when you present a technique to them and allow them to learn it. I've seen well-meaning coaches interrupt a drill training session to offer detailed instruction. Sure, offer advice and correction if you see something an athlete is doing wrong and positive comments to help them work harder, but don't over-coach your athletes.

Some people mistake realism for resistance and non-cooperation. Some drills call for total realism (Open-ended Drills) while others call for varying degrees of cooperation. For instance, a group of judo athletes can randori, with the partners going only 50% (what Bryan Potter calls "smiling randori") and prevent the randori session from becoming a mini-tournament. This drill is a realistic, open-ended drill, but has a good level of cooperation so that learning can still take place.

Drill training is effective if you use it wisely. Drilling, like anything, can be overdone or done incorrectly. Remember also that drill training has to have a purpose. Don't simply invent a "drill" because it involves a bunch of different body movements. There has to be a reason why you're doing what you're doing. Don't simply go through the motions, but instead, go through the motions with a purpose.

Often a coach can teach an underlying movement, skill or tactic by using a well-planned drill or game. This is where, as I mentioned before, a drill can have more than one use, even though it has a specific purpose. An example is when teaching a throw using a crash pad not only teaches the mechanics of the particular throw, it also teaches the athletes to follow through with more force and control since the guy getting thrown is landing on 8 inches of foam and not on the regular mat. This element of safety is important to successful learning and successful training results. Learning how to throw hard with force and control is part of a mechanically and fundamentally sound throwing technique.

Drill Training Offers Variety

Drills and games offer a variety of training opportunities and I often use games to help warm up my athletes as well drill on specific skills. Don't be fooled into thinking games aren't hard training. I often like to tell my athletes that I "fool them into training hard" by having them play some training games during a workout. Training games work great for kids but adults like to do them as well. Several good training games are included in this book.

Ever since working with Lou Moyerman and Bob Corwin in 1985 at a U.S. Olympic Training Center camp in Lake Placid, New York, I've used "Judo Circuits." You can call them "Jujitsu Circuits" or "Grappling Circuits." The name really doesn't matter, but what does matter is the great training effect you get from them.

Basically, judo circuits are several exercises or drills done immediately after one another for a specific amount of time or repetitions. An example is Grappler A does a set of uchikomi on Grappler B for 30 seconds, then Grappler B does his set of uchikomi for 30 seconds. Immediately after this set of uchikomi, Grappler A does another set of a specified drill for 30 seconds with Grappler B following when it's his turn. They would go through five specific exercises or drills that make up the circuit.

String drills together to form a circuit. Here are some circuits I like to use for my athletes.

Standing Skills Circuit

   1. Forward Throwing Uchikomi (non-moving)

   2 . Hip Block Drill

   3. Rear Throw Uchikomi (non-moving)

   4. Grip-fighting Drill

   5. Favorite Throw Uchikomi (moving)

Fitness Circuit

1. Side Hopping Drill

2. Crunches (or Sit-ups)

3. Vertical Jumps

4. Sit-through Drill

5. Push-ups

Judo Circuits are "interval training" in its purest form and is an excellent fitness and skill program for serious athletes. Interval training is an intense period of exercise followed by an equal period of time for rest. Usually done in sets, interval training develops high levels of fitness and conditioning. You can use a set of Judo Circuits as an intensive part of your workout after you have done some milder warm-ups or as a "finish" drill after your training session is completed. Judo Circuits can be intense and you should use them when you're in good shape and not for recreational, novice or untrained athletes. However, this is fantastic and serious training and I recommend using them.

One important note is that when doing Judo Circuits, the athletes should know how to do each drill or exercise in the circuit so they can get the most out of the drill and immediately move from one drill to the next so that the effectiveness of the circuit won't be diminished.

Drill Training Only Works If You Do It

Drill training works, plain and simple. It provides structured, disciplined training to anyone who uses it. You can know all the drills in the world, but if you don't use them and use them on a regular basis, you won't get any benefit from them. Any experienced coach or athlete will quickly spot a grappler who doesn't know how to drill train. He's always the guy in the workout that resists everything you do, is tight and rigid in his body movement and doesn't seem to understand that training is a cooperative undertaking and not a fight for survival. In other words, you have to use drill training on a consistent and regular basis in order to make the technical progress necessary to perform at advanced or elite levels, whether it's a competitive grappling sport or self-defense.

The drills and games in this book are ones that I've used as a coach and have seen other coaches and athletes use as well. There are a lot of drills you can use and this book is intended to stimulate your thought and offer some new ideas on how to drill efficiently. I also want to convince anyone who doesn't use drill training why drill training is vital to your success as an athlete or coach. It's my hope that coaches and athletes can use this book for many years to come as a source of good, reliable information. Feel free to change any of the drills or games in this book so they work better for you.

Including drill training as part of your regular routine will make a major difference, and for the better, in your results as a athlete in any combat sport or martial art.

SAMPLE DRILL TRAINING WORKOUTS

By using drill training as part of your overall training program, you'll get more out of your workouts and be far more efficient in how you use your time on the mat or in the training room. I'm including some sample workout routines you can follow that include drill training here, but remember, it's your practice and your time, so alter any advice I offer to make it suit your needs better. Also take into account where you are in your training cycle. While this book doesn't discuss periodization, the type and intensity of workout, how often you work out and other factors have to be taken into account. These lesson plans are general in nature and I'm offering them as a guide on how to include and use drill training as part of your regular training time.

Basic Grappler's Workout

Here's a plan for a disciplined and performance directed workout for any grappling activity, whether it's judo, sambo or submission grappling:

- Warm-up (About 10 minutes training time.)

- Warm-up games or exercises

- Functional stretching

- Breakfalls and tumbling

- Drill Training (About 20-30 minutes of training time.) Do a variety of gripping, throwing and groundfighting drills with each drill going about 5 to 7 minutes each (on the average).

- Skill Training (About 20 minutes training time). The coach will teach a new move or technique or work on one that has been taught before and add new elements or link new skills to it. Allow the athletes to spend a good deal of time working on this move or series of moves the coach has presented.

• Open Training (About 30 minutes). This is time for randori, practice matches or simply allowing the athletes to work on what they want. Some may want to get more time doing crash pad throwing or work on a specific skill they want to learn better. The coach goes around the mat to see that everyone is working hard and smart.

Adult Judo/Jujitsu/Sambo Workout

This routine is for advanced and elite athletes. This isn't a workout for brand new people or someone who is not is good shape. It's a serious workout. This workout takes about 2 hours. You can cut down the time for each phase of training to make it fit into a 90-minute time slot if you wish.

• Warm-up (About 10 minutes training time.)

1. Jog around the mat or do some mild calisthenics for about a minute to start the body warming up.

2. Do some breakfalls, rolls or tumbling. Breakfalls are important for safety so they should be practiced regularly, but the rolling, falling and tumbling action of the breakfalls (and other tumbling movements) toughens the body up for the upcoming training session.

3. Warm-up Game (Riders and Horses, Side Hopping, Roll Around like a Ball or other game; just do one game because this is still a warm-up and you want to prepare your body for stretching.)

4. Functional stretching should be done for a brief period, but as long as needed by the athletes.

• Drill Training: (About 20-30 minutes training time for all the drills.) This is a time when the athletes work on moves and skills they already know and want to get better at. The coach will offer encouragement and advice as needed, but not detailed instruction. Most of these drills are short and intense in time. I usually allow 3 to 5 minutes per drill, and while you may think this isn't enough time on each drill, remember that drill training has a cumulative effect and if you consistently do these drills every practice or on a regular basis, they add up.

1. Do grip fighting drills and Grip Randori (go about 4 or 5 rounds of 30-40 seconds per round of grip fighting). The emphasis should be on aggressive gripping and grip breaking and controlling the mat space, body movement and tempo of the opponent. This isn't randori where you try to throw your partner, it's aggressive, grip randori where you try to beat him to the grip and control him with your grip

2. Throwing Uchikomi and Moving Drills:

 • Static Uchikomi: Each partner does 5 sets of 10 of his favorite throw.

 • Hip Block Drill: Have one partner attack the other for 30 seconds with a forward throw with the defending partner doing hip blocks to work on his defense against a throw.

 • Crash Pad Throws: Allow about 10 minutes for the athletes to throw each other on the crash pads.

3. Mat (Groundfighting) Uchikomi:

 • Spinning Cross-body Armlock: Do in sets of 3 each with total cooperation to develop the skill. Allow about 4 minutes for this drill so each athlete will be able to do about 30 to 40 repetitions.

 • Far Arm-Near Leg Breakdown: Have the athletes do as many good breakdowns on each other in 30-second rounds. Go about 2 rounds each. Again, this is a skill drill, so have athletes cooperate 100% with each other or the coach can instruct them to offer varying degrees of resistance.

 • Breakdown to Choke Drill: Allow your athletes to use their favorite breakdown to their favorite choke or strangle. Have them take turns and allow several minutes (up to 5 minute). I usually have the guys perform 2 or 3 breakdowns, then let their partner do his 2 or 3 and repeat this for about 5 minutes. Again, total cooperation is a good idea so the skill can be developed.

• Leg Lace Drill for Leglocks: This is a good, safe way to drill on leglocks. Do this drill for about 2 or 3 30-second rounds.

• Guard Drill Training: Allow the athletes about 5 minutes to work on their favorite guard passes, rollovers and sweeps and other aspects of fighting from this position. The coach should go around and offer advice. This isn't a time for teaching new moves or techniques; it's a time for drilling on the moves the athletes already know.

• Lock Ins: This is a pin escape drill. Have the athletes go 2 30-second rounds with total resistance.

• Skill Training: (About 15 minutes training time.) This is the time the coach uses to teach new skills. Allow about 15 to 20 minutes for this phase of the workout. Be sure to give the athletes plenty of time to work on the techniques.

• Open Practice: (About 30 minutes training time.) Have the group go through randori training (practice matches). I usually have the athletes go through about five 5-minute rounds of randori, allowing a minute or two between rounds.

Randori Workout (Called Various Names by Different Coaches)

• Warm-up (About 10 minutes training time.)

• Various games or exercises to warm the body up for stretching.

• Functional stretching.

• Tumbling or breakfalls.

• Groundfighting Drill/Randori (About 20 minutes training time). Have the athletes pair up and go about five 3-minute rounds on groundfighting only.

• Standing to Ground Randori (About 30-40 minutes training time). Have the athletes go a good number of rounds from the standing position to start. While some judo coaches only have their guys use throws in this type of randori and don't go into groundfighting, I believe that in a real match you always follow your opponent to the mat after you've thrown him, so this should be done in training as well. I will generally have the athletes go about six or seven 5-minute rounds of randori. The coach supervises and times the workout.

WARM UPS, STRETCHING AND COOL DOWNS

Every effective training session must have some time allowed for three phases of training:

1. A warm up, where you physically warm the muscles of your body up in preparation for the stretching to follow as well as the harder training later in the workout.

2. A stretching routine that is functional in nature. By functional, I mean that the stretches you do should relate to what we do in grappling and martial arts. Stretch to your normal range of motion and try to increase your range of motion safely and slowly until you believe you have reached the most efficient range of motion possible. Stretching is vital to avoid injuries and to be able to perform the many movements your body is required to do in our rough and tumble world of grappling.

3. After each workout, spend a few minutes doing some cool down exercises, drills or games. A good cool down is to do some light calisthenics such as jumping jacks, or maybe a light jog around the perimeter of the mat. From time to time, I have my athletes give each other a light 1-minute massage to help get the soreness out of the muscles.

Your warm ups should somehow relate to the sport you are doing. It makes it more enjoyable and effective if the warm up ties in with what you'll be doing later in the workout.

SHOW UP IN SHAPE

Your training off the mat is important! If you only think training on the mat is all you need, you won't ever improve. Your fitness training off the mat should include regular workouts of both cardio training and training. It's important that when you train in the weight room, you train to be a fighter, not a bodybuilder or powerlifter. You don't have to have a beautiful body to win fights. Most of the best grapplers and MMA fighters I've ever seen have been well built and have a "fighter's physique."

Functional training off the mat is necessary for success. You can't perform the skills of judo, jujitsu, sambo, MMA or any combat sport at an advanced or elite level unless you are physically able to do so. Physical ability is necessary to have excellent technical ability. Functional training is done in 3 areas:

1. Strength training. You have to be strong physically. The stronger you are, the better. I don't mean to imply that you rely on brute strength and not skill to win, but the combination of strength and skill is better than only strength or only skill.

2. Cardio training. Aerobic fitness is vital to success in any form of sport combat. If you gas, you won't be able to perform the skills you want or need to do to win. Not only that, you will be far less likely to want to fight or compete if you aren't in good cardio shape. Like the great football coach Vince Lombardi said, "Physical weakness makes cowards of us all."

3. Flexibility training. You don't have to be as flexible as a gymnast, but you should be flexible enough to perform the skills of your sport. As with strength and cardio fitness, the more functionally flexible you are, the better you will be able to perform the technical skills.

Your diet is part of all this as well. The old saying "You are what you eat" is true. Also, if you have to cut weight, do it smart and do it gradually. Crash diets only weaken you and you won't be able to compete effectively. Remember, you're not training for a weight loss contest; you're training for a judo, jujitsu, MMA or other type of tournament or match. If you're training for self-defense reasons, a healthy diet is fundamental to a healthy lifestyle and overall approach to training. Being soft or overweight isn't an option if you have to ever defend yourself in a real fight.

THREE ELEMENTS OF SUCCESS

There are three essential elements that lead to success in every form of martial art. The concept of Shingitai explains these concepts very well. This approach to training has been used for years by martial artists as well as athletes in other sports and activities. As a member and supporter of the Shingitai Jujitsu Association, these three concepts or elements form the basis of how I have approached training in the martial arts for my entire career as an athlete and as a coach. The three concepts of Shin, Gi and Tai, when used in proper proportion to each other, form the basis of what I'm talking about.

Shin (Fighting Heart, Mental Approach)

This Japanese word translates to mean "fighting heart." To be successful in a fighting sport or martial discipline, you must have the will to not only win, but also enjoy the rough and tumble activity you are engaged in. This doesn't mean you need to be the toughest guy in the world, but it does mean you should be tough enough to get the job done. Often when two skilled grapplers are matched up, the better fighter will win. A grappler or fighter must enjoy the challenge of fighting and love the competition. The words of the famous lawman of the old west Bat Masterson are true, "It's not always the fastest or most accurate, it's the most willing."

Gi (Applied Technical Ability)

This Japanese word translates to mean "applied technical ability." This is what skill is. You have to be skillful and know how and why your skills work best for you. You can win by brute force, luck or other factors for only so long and against only a limited level of competition. My first sambo coach, Maurice Allen, told me, "Make the technique work for you." If you want to be a champion, you have to be able to apply the techniques and make them work for you.

Tai (Body, Physical Fitness)

This word actually means "body" and anything relating to the body. For our purposes, it means physical fitness. "Show up in shape" is a phrase you should live by as a grappler. The great football coach Vince Lombardi said, "Physical weakness makes cowards of us all." If you want to perform any skill against a resisting, serious, physically fit and skilled opponent, you must be physically capable of doing it.

TRAINING RULES

It's important for all coaches and instructors to have some guidelines, rules, or whatever you want to call them to set the tone for practice at your club. You will want to look at your own situation and develop your own set of rules, but whatever you do, develop a set of training rules and follow them.

1. Train Realistically and Correctly. Work on skills that really work. Develop your skills so that they will work in real situations with a high ratio of success. This is true for sport jujitsu, submission grappling or self-defense jujitsu applications. Train on correctly done skills. Don't do a drill to simply get it over. Correct practice produces correct results. Whatever you train on, make sure it's realistic and effective.

2. Follow Through. Make sure that you continue to drive into the throw so that your opponent lands as hard or as soft as you want and in a controlled situation. When you throw him, follow immediately with a groundfighting move to further immobilize him or force him to submit.

3. Link Your Techniques Together. This means you shouldn't think of a throw or hold as an isolated movement. Work on setting your opponent up, how to grab him, body posture, tempo change and other factors to better control him and control the situation.

4. Develop Physical Strength and Endurance in Addition to Jujitsu Skills. Your jujitsu will work better if you're in good shape, plain and simple.

5. Work Out in a Regular Routine. Be disciplined. You have to concentrate on what you are doing at practice. Be willing to attend special clinics, tournaments and other events that can make you better. But, most importantly, show up to practice on a regular basis.

6. Work Hard! Don't merely go through the motions. The more intense the workout, the better for you and the more you get out of it. Face the fact that you are engaged in a contact sport where you will take some lumps and dish them out as well. You will take abuse in practice or competition, so deal with it and it will make you better.

7. Respect Your Training Partners. Don't beat them up in practice and remember that you are all on the same team. My good friend, Harry Parker, used to say, "The best piece of training equipment in the dojo is another human being."

8. Practice the Use of Tactics. Put yourself (while training) into situations that will actually come up in a real situation, whether it is sport jujitsu or in a self-defense practice. You want to have a high ratio of success in any situation, so study the situations that can arise and train accordingly.

9. Don't Neglect Any Phase of Training. You may dislike some aspect of training, but don't neglect it. Work on your weak points as well as your strong points. We all have particular things we like to do and will do these things well. On the other hand, we all have particular things we don't like to do but must persist and make sure that we can perform them with enough success to make them work when we need them.

10. Develop Skills on Both Right and Left Sides. This doesn't mean that you have to do all skills with equal ability on both sides. It's not always possible to perform a movement equally well on both sides. Everyone has a dominant side, but try to develop skill on both sides so that you can adapt to just about any situation that may come up. You may find that the way you perform a particular throw, strike or hold on the right side is different than the way you do it on the left side. As long as they are both effective, it's okay.

THE SELF-DEFENSE ATHLETE

Every combat sport or form of martial art is descended from the actual military training and fighting that every culture and country on Earth has or has ever had. Why do you think they call this stuff "martial arts?" Martial means military and the military's main job is to fight wars. As a coach, I have a lot of young men and women who are active or reserve members of the military. The people we have in all branches of our military are what can be described as "athletes in uniform." These people are athletes in every sense of the word. Fighting somebody in a judo tournament is nothing to fighting in a real war and the training necessary to win wars is just as physical, just as mental and just as tough as what it takes to be a champion grappler.

In a similar sense, my friend John Saylor coined the phrase "self-defense athlete" and this is an accurate description of the people who train in the martial arts for the most basic reason of all, and that's to win in a real fight. The fighters who train in Krav Maga and other martial arts where there is no competitive outlet are just as much athletes as the fighters who train in a wrestling room, dojo or gym.

If you're a self-defense athlete, the drills in this book can be valuable to you as well. It's my belief that the skills in a good, effective combat sport can be used as good, effective combat. Quoting my friend John Saylor again, "Jujitsu is first and foremost a fighting art." If you always remember your roots as a martial artist or grappler, you will always be able to use the skills you develop in sport combat in the real thing.

THE COACH'S JOB

Every training session needs someone who is in charge. This is why a good coach is important to your success as an athlete. If you don't have a coach to run the practice or workout, assign someone to be the person timing the drills and supervising the training session.

Every coach should have, and use, a stopwatch. It's an important tool for you. It's also important to have a well-stocked first-aid kit with ice or instant cold packs nearby as well. You never know when a training injury will occur and you need to be ready. You want to practice hard, but you want to practice safely as well. Training injuries are nothing to brag about.

Sometimes when training, the best coach on the mat is your training partner. Good teammates and workout partners will help each other through rough spots and point out errors as well as offer encouragement for a job well done. Also, it's a good idea to video tape your workouts once in a while to see how you are progressing.

Bryan Potter is timing the guys in a drill at a typical workout.

I recommend that you read my book COACHING ON THE MAT if you are interested in more information on effective coaching. Additionally, there are many good books on the market about coaching. Even if you don't plan on becoming a coach, learning more about the subject of effective teaching will only make you a better athlete. It's sage advice that, "Those who teach learn twice." If you actually teach someone a skill, you always learn that skill better.

PLAN YOUR TRAINING AND YOUR GOALS

It's wise to plan out your training sessions, both long-term and short-term. It doesn't matter what the subject is that you want to excel in; you need to have a plan to achieve your goals.

A long-term goal of what you want to accomplish as an athlete is necessary. From that long-term goal, break it down to what you want to accomplish in five years, four years, three years, two years, one year, then what you want to accomplish this year. Be firm, yet flexible. If you have to make changes, then do it, but always keep your goals in mind and look at how these changes will alter them. Use periodization or cycle training to efficiently train and to meet your goals. Periodization is the practice of breaking down specific times of the year into "cycles" of training so that you don't become stale and get the most out of your training. There are many good books on the market about periodization, but my friend John Saylor wrote one of the best I've read, called STRENGTH AND CONDITIONING SECRETS OF THE WORLD'S GREATEST FIGHTERS. Although there are no "secrets" in this great book, it is filled with lots of useful information on training, including periodization. To get a copy, go to John's web site at www.JohnSaylor-SJA.com.

You also have to make choices in life. How you live your life is important to your success as an athlete or fighter. Smoking, excessive drinking, a poor diet, and running around with people who make bad choices won't make you a champion, no matter how hard you workout in the dojo or gym. You don't have to be a saint, but self-discipline can be your best friend. The choices you make determine your success and you can't separate your daily life from your life as an athlete or grappler.

Plan out the tournaments or matches for a year in advance if possible. If you're a collegiate or high school wrestler, you have a season of duals and tournaments that is planned out. Not all grapplers or combat athletes have this available to them, so talk with your coach and work out your own "season." Try to plan out what tournaments you want to compete in locally and regionally and what you are shooting for on the national or international level. Always compete for a reason. If the reason you're competing in a particular tournament is for fun, great, but if the reason you're competing in another tournament is to qualify for an international team, then you know exactly what you have to do. As an athlete, I always asked' "What's in it for me?" Then, later, as a coach, I always asked; "What's in it for my athletes?" You have to be selfish for yourself as an athlete, and as a coach, you have to be selfish for your team. Some people may think this sounds harsh, but it's true if you want to excel at anything you do, especially in our world of grappling and fighting.

Specifically, when you get to the dojo or gym, you should have a good idea what you want to do that evening. Plan out the drills you will use and what you want to work on that night. Talk to your coach and discuss your training with him on a regular basis. Whatever you do, make it a point to have some structured training, including drill training as a major part of your workout. The drills presented in this book are effective and ones that I have used and have seen used by other coaches and athletes. Use this book as a good reference and consult other sources of information as well. Remember, the best way to plan out a drill is to look at what happens in a real match, break it down to its elemental parts and invent drills for it. There are so many different situations that come up in a match or real fight; it's almost easy inventing drills to meet the needs of the particular situation if you think of it in this analytical way.

Be optimistic and realistic. If your goal is to make the Olympic team, be realistic in your approach to achieving this goal. Realize that your life will change forever if you do this and be ready to make those changes. If you want to be a pro MMA fighter and have never done any sport or form of martial art where you were physically pushed to your limits, you better "get with the program" as Rene Pommerelle used to say. For this reason, it's best to set a long-term goal, but focus on the mid-term and short-term goals and do everything you can to meet that long-term goal.

SECTION TWO:
Fitness Drills

"I always say to myself before a match; I worked too hard to lose to this guy"
Jim Martin, Pan American Games Champion in Sambo

Breakfalls, Cartwheels and Tumbling

Purpose: Tumbling and breakfalls teach safety, coordination, plyometric strength and just about every good thing you can imagine for any martial art. Doing breakfalls not only reinforces good habits of falling safely, it actually toughens up the body for the punishment it will take later in the practice. Cartwheels and other tumbling skills are excellent for all grapplers and martial arts athletes.

Age Level: All ages.

How It's Done: Do breakfalls and tumbling as part of your warm-up before your stretching routine, especially if you're a novice. It's a good way to physically warm the muscles up in your body so your stretching can be more effective. It's a good way to get your body ready for the rough and tumble training that will follow. Do rolling falls, cartwheels or round offs down the length of the mat.

Knowing how to fall properly is an important part of safety in training. It's especially important for novices to learn how to do breakfalls correctly and practice them on a regular basis. Breakfall drills also help toughen the body up for harder training later in the workout.

Tumbling skills such as cartwheels and round offs are important to drill on as well. Tumbling teaches better agility, coordination and how to control your body better. Tumbling drills are also a great way to warm up your body before you start your functional stretching during the first part of your workout.

Side Hopping Drill

Purpose: This is a plyometric drill that emphasizes agility training and aerobic fitness.

Age Level: All ages can do this drill.

How It's Done: A pair of training partners does this drill. The idea is to hop over your partner's legs as quickly as possible in the allotted time. This drill can be timed by the coach or done in a set number of repetitions. Count each time the hopping athlete touches the mat at a repetition. I usually have my athletes do one set of 30 seconds each as part of their initial warm-up. It can be done with the bottom athlete sitting with his legs extended and together, with his legs extended and wide or with the bottom athlete on his hands and knees in a tight ball. The hopping athlete can do this on both legs or on one leg.

Legs Extended and Together Variation: Drew is ready to start the drill with Bryan's legs extended and together. Drew hops over Bryan's knees.

Drew has hopped over Bryan's legs.

Drew immediately hops back over Bryan's legs.

Legs Extended and Spread Variation: Drew hops over each of Bryan's legs in this variation for more agility training.

Drew hops as quickly as possible making sure to not touch Bryan's legs.

Drew hops over Bryan's leg and will hop back as many times as possible to complete the drill.

Partner on All Fours Variation: Bryan is on his hands and knees in a tight ball and Drew will hop over him. This forces Drew to hop higher for a better plyometric training effect.

This is a good warm-up drill and develops plyometric power that is so important to any grappling sport.

Drew hops back over Bryan and does as may repetitions as possible in the time allowed by the coach. As I said before, I usually time this drill for 30 seconds per athlete and let the team compete with each other to see who does the most hops in the 30 seconds.

Shrimping Drill

Purpose: Shrimping is an important skill in groundfighting and this drill should be done on a regular basis. This is a great warm-up exercise.

Age Level: All ages.

How It's Done: Start by lying on your back and roll to one side and curl up. Push against the mat with your feet and extend your legs. This action propels you forward on the mat. Roll to the other side as soon as you fully extend your legs and repeat the exercise.

The team is shrimping across the mat as part of their warm-up for the evening's practice.

Bryan starts the shrimp drill by laying on his back as shown.

Bryan rolls to his left side and starts to push against the mat with both of his feet.

Bryan pushes hard against the mat with both feet propelling him. He will quickly roll to the other side and repeat this movement.

Climb The Tree Drill

Purpose: This drill develops strength, agility and balance.

Age Level: All ages can do this drill.

How It's Done: One partner (the "tree") stands with his feet planted wide and can place his hands on his knees for added support if he wishes, while the other athlete will hop onto him and climb all over him. The "climber" has a goal to climb completely around the "tree" without falling to the mat. This is a great agility and strength drill for the climber and an excellent strength drill for the athlete who is the tree. It's a lot of fun to do and I recommend this for everyone, but especially for kids. The coach can time this drill and give each climber 30 to 40 seconds to climb the tree. If the climber falls to the mat, he simply gets up and starts climbing again until his time is up.

Drew has hopped up on Chris and is ready to climb around his body. Notice that Chris is well balanced in his stance and posture.

Chas is climbing his tree, in this case, Jarrod, who is standing strong. Bryan is conducting the drill and has his stopwatch in hand.

Chas continues to climb around Jarrod with the goal being not to fall to the mat.

Good Morning Drill

Purpose: Develop low back and leg strength as well as the ability to pick an opponent off the mat who has you in a submission technique. In many combat sports, the bottom grappler will attempt a submission technique from the guard position. This drill teaches athletes how to immediately pick an opponent up off the mat and nullify or break the submission technique. This is similar to the "Good Morning" exercise done in the weight room.

Age Level: Adults and Older Teens. This is a strenuous low back exercise and should only be done by athletes who have adequate low back strength.

How It's Done: The standing athlete (A) has his legs wide apart and had a strong base with his lower body. Athlete A bends over and picks up his partner who is lying on his back with his legs wrapped around the waist of the standing athlete. The standing athlete either grabs his partner's jacket lapels or grabs under his partner's armpits and holds his back. The standing athlete picks up the bottom athlete and swings him up. The standing athlete then lowers his partner to the mat with control. This is done repeatedly. The coach can do this as a timed drill with each athlete doing as many repetitions as possible and with good control in an allotted time (I use 30 seconds). The athletes can also do this in sets of 10 (or any number) repetitions. This isn't a drill for novice athletes or children and the coach should emphasize that the athletes use good lifting form to avoid straining the lower back.

Bryan bends over and grabs Nikolay's jacket as shown. It's important for Bryan to bend his legs slightly, much in the same way he would if he did this movement in the weight room. Nikolay, on the bottom, is also holding on and grabs Bryan's jacket.

Bryan picks Nikolay off the mat as shown.

Bryan lowers Nikolay to the mat with control and repeats the movement.

Rolling Drill

Purpose: This is a good warm up drill and teaches the athletes to stay round and relaxed on the mat.

Age Level: All ages.

How It's Done: One grappler gets on all fours and balls up as tightly as possible. His partner gets on his hands and knees and rolls him around the mat in all directions. This is an enjoyable, physical drill that is a lot of fun and a good warm up. I time this drill for 30 to 40 seconds and let the athletes go 2 or 3 rounds with a different partner each round.

The team is doing the Rolling Drill as part of their initial warm up before stretching. Stay as round as possible. Both partners cooperate 100% as this is a fun drill that gets the body ready for more training.

Kirt has rolled Erik completely over his head and shoulders in this drill.

Guard Ball

Purpose: This drill is a great aerobic fitness drill as well as a strength drill and is a fun and effective warm-up. Also, just as important, this drill teaches the bottom athlete (the one in the guard and "guarding" the ball) to protect his middle area and not let his opponent get past his legs. This drill teaches the top grappler to aggressively get past his opponent's legs and hips passing his guard.

Age level: All ages.

How It's Done: The bottom grappler holds tightly onto a ball (I prefer a medicine ball, but you can use any ball, or even a belt that is knotted up) and holds it to his chest and stomach. His job is to keep his partner from taking the ball from him. An important rule in this drill is that the bottom grappler can't roll over onto his front and hide the ball from his partner (making it too difficult to take away). The top grappler can try any way he can to wrench the ball free from his partner's hold. The coach can give each athlete an allotted time. I usually run this drill in 30 to 40 second rounds. If the top athlete takes the ball from the bottom athlete, simply start the drill over again with the same athlete holding the ball until time runs out. Another variation is when the top athlete manages to take the ball from the bottom athlete, the athletes trade places and restart the drill with the other athlete now guarding the ball.

Jarrod, on the bottom, is guarding his ball from Roy.

Bryan is trying to pry the ball loose from Chris' hold. This drill is a lot of fun and is a great way to warm your athletes up. The drill also teaches important skills in fighting from and in the guard position.

British Bulldog

Purpose: A great game to warm the group up and it teaches aggressive behavior on the mat. This is also a good drill for learning how to do breakdowns and keep an opponent from breaking you down. This is a popular game and goes by several names, but I always heard it called British Bulldog.

Age Level: All ages, but especially great for kids.

How It's Done: The coach has the group line up on one side of the mat on their hands and knees. The coach then assigns one or two athletes to be the "bulldog". The athletes who crawl on hands and knees back and forth across the mat are the "poodles" and the bulldogs try to turn the poodles crawling back and forth onto their backs. If an athlete is turned onto his back, he's no longer a poodle and becomes a bulldog and can attack the others. Poodles can resist being turned over but can't help each other. When everyone has been turned onto his or her back and is a bulldog the game is over. The last person to be made into a bulldog wins. Some basic rules are that bulldogs can gang up on one poodle, so 2 or more bulldogs can try to turn a poodle over onto his back. Another rule is that poodles are on their own; no other poodles can help them. All they do is crawl back and forth on the mat and do everything they can to resist or avoid being turned over. If calling somebody a poodle isn't macho enough, call them anything you want, but no matter what you call them, this is a fun game and a good workout.

Here's how British Bulldog starts. Javier is the bulldog and it's his job to turn his training partners onto their backs. When someone is turned over, he or she becomes a bulldog and joins Javier in trying to turn other over.

Here's British Bulldog in action. Chad's been turned over and is now a bulldog and is going after Nick. It's a lot of fun for all ages and is a great game that keeps the group training hard in an enjoyable way. Here's a good example of how you can train hard and still have a good time.

Riders and Horses

Purpose: This is a fun game that teaches aggression and is a total body workout.

Age Level: Kids, but adults like this game as well.

How It's Done: One athlete is the "horse" and the other is the "rider." The idea of this game is for the riders to pull one another off he horses. Only the riders can pull other people and the horses simply serve as the horse. When there is only one rider and horse left, they are the winning team.

The riders try to pull as many other riders off their horses as possible. The last rider and horse left is the winning team.

Mat Tag

Purpose: This is a good warm up game, especially for kids.

Age Level: Kids.

How It's Done: Basically, this is a tag game only with the players on hands and knees. Having them do this game on hands and knees makes them work harder. There are 2 basic ways to play this game. The first is to have one player be "it" and when he tags another player, he becomes the new "it." The coach can time the game when it's done this way. The second way is when "it" tags another player, he becomes "it" also and when everyone has been tagged, the game is over.

Bryan is "it" and is about to start the game.

This is a non-stop game and a lot of fun for kids, but adults like it once in a while as well.

Toilet Ball

Purpose: This game is a lot of fun and a good warm up for all age groups. It's a very physical game and keeps the group moving the entire time it's played.

Age Level: All ages.

How It's Done: This is a keep-away game where there are 2 teams. You must throw, pass or hand off the ball to another teammate and he does the same to another. When one team makes 10 completions, they win. The opposing team can bat down the ball, try to steal it, try to incept the pass or get the ball away from the other team any way possible and make 10 completions to each other as well. I usually have a rule where the athletes aren't allowed to tackle each other or get real rough. The coach should count out loud each completed pass to keep the score straight. A player can't throw it to another and have him throw it right back (no back and forth passes). This game got its name from the judo athletes at the U.S. Olympic Training Center where they used it as a great warm up before their workouts. One day, they wanted to play this keep-away game, but didn't have a ball, so one of the athletes went to the bathroom and took a roll of toilet paper and wrapped it with athletic tape. Thus, toilet ball was born.

The guys teamed up as shirts and skins and are playing toilet ball.

Sumo

Purpose: This is a good game to teach aggressive grappling. It's great for strength, balance and everything you want in a rough and tumble drill.

Age Level: Kids, but adults like this as well.

How It's Done: The winner stays up in this game. Make a circle on the mat with judo belts. If one athlete touches the mat with anything other than the bottom of his feet or goes out of the circle, he's the loser. The 2 grapplers squat and bend over, tapping the mat a couple of time with their hands to signal the start of the match. You can throw your opponent, pick him up and carry him out of the circle or push him down in the same way the sport of sumo is done. (No slapping or dirty stuff; this is for fun!)

Here's the start of the sumo game.

Kolden's picked Derrick up and is going to put him down outside the ring to win the match.

Circle Drill

Purpose: This drill teaches good, aggressive foot sweeps and is great for balance. It's a tough fitness drill as well and really works the cardio.

Age Level: Older kids, teens and adults.

How It's Done: Form a circle with everyone and have each athlete hold the lapel of the grappler next to him on each side. At the coach's signal, they all try to foot sweep or throw each other down. When one athlete hits the mat with anything other than his feet, he's considered "down" and the coach stops the drill momentarily to allow the athletes to grip each other's lapels again and start over. This is a lot of fun and can go for a long time if you make the circle too big. It's ideal to have no more than 10 athletes in a circle to keep the game going faster.

Start the Circle Drill with everyone holding each other's lapels forming a circle.

This photo shows the athletes really going at it and trying hard to foot sweep each other. Sometimes, more than one guy will hit the mat, and if this takes place, everyone who goes down is put out of the game.

Belt Jump Drill

Purpose: This drill is good for developing plyometric power.

Age Level: Kids and teens.

How It's Done: The coach or a teammate lays out several belts on the mat at varying distances from each other. The jumper will do a standing (not running) long jump over each belt and hop between the belts on the mat as fast as possible. If the jumper touches a belt, falls or can't jump over the next belt, he's out of the game. The coach will remove one belt at a time making the distance between the belts longer. This makes the jumper jump further each time.

Derrick is ready to jump over each belt as quickly as he can.

Derrick jumps or hops as quickly as possible over the belts.

Kolden removed a belt, making Derrick jump farther.

Pick Up and Walk Drill

Purpose: This drill teaches good throwing or takedown form and develops overall strength to throw an opponent. This is a good strength drill and offers a different way of working on the muscles that you use in throwing.

Age Level: Adults and older teens.

How It's Done: You and your partner are standing on one side of the mat and you pick him up with a double leg or other throw or takedown. After you pick him up and load him onto your shoulder or chest, walk him to the other side of the mat. Put him down on his feet and he will do the same drill on you, walking you back. Do this back and forth for a specific time or set number of repetitions.

Bryan picks up Nikolay with a front double leg making sure to use good form.

Bryan picks Nikolay up and loads him as he starts to walk forward. Bryan will carry Nikolay to the opposite side of the mat and put him down. Nikolay will then pick Bryan up and carry him back.

Leap Frog Drill

Purpose: This drill is a good warm up and develops plyometric power from the jumping.

Age Level: All ages.

How It's Done: One partner is behind the other and jumps over his back, then crawls through between his partner's legs and repeats the drill. I usually time the athletes for 30-second rounds. Make it competitive and see how many repetitions each athlete can do in the allotted time.

Drew is ready to jump over Bryan. Bryan is bent over so Drew can jump over him.

This is a good plyometric drill. Explosive power is necessary for good skill in throws and takedowns.

Drew lands and crawls back through Bryan's legs.

Drew has crawled through and will repeat the drill.

Seated Partner Crunches

Purpose: This is a good warm up and develops the abdominals and lower back.

Age Level: All ages.

How It's Done: This is a variation of an old-fashioned sit-up and is good for abdominal training.

One partner sits on his buttocks and holds his partner's legs for stability.

The partner doing the crunches does as many as possible in 30-second rounds.

Standing Partner Crunches

Purpose: This drill develops strength for both athletes. The one holding his partner develops leg, back and shoulder strength and the one doing the crunches develops abdominal, lower back and hip strength.

Age Level: Adults and teens.

How It's Done: The athlete doing the crunches jumps up and wraps his legs around his partner who catches him and holds him. The athlete doing the crunches curls all the way up and extends all the way down for full effect of this drill. Time them in 30-seconds rounds or have each athlete do a specific number of repetitions.

Drew has jumped up on Bryan and wrapped his legs around him. Bryan is holding Drew at his belt.

Drew extends as far as he can with Bryan holding on tight to keep him from falling to the mat.

Drew curls all the way up to complete the crunch, and then repeats the exercise.

Belt Tug of War

Purpose: This game develops strength and is a lot of fun, especially for kids.

Age Level: Kids.

How It's Done: Just like any game of tug of war, only we use our belts in this version of the game. If you pull your opponent over the belt laid on the mat, you win. Go the best 2 out of 3 and switch partners.

Bryan and Drew tugging away in this fun game which is a great way to warm the group up for more serious training. This is a game that can be played once in a while, and can be used by the coach as a reward for the kids in a judo or jujitsu class.

SECTION THREE:
Skill Drills

"Practice doesn't make perfect. Perfect practice makes perfect."
Vince Lombardi, Football Coach

Matwork Uchikomi
(Also Called Newaza Uchikomi & Groundfighting Uchikomi)

Purpose: This develops excellent skill in breaking an opponent down and immediately finishing him with a pin, choke, armlock or leglock. It's a fundamental and important drill and you should spend a good amount of time each practice or workout doing Matwork Uchikomi training.

Age Level: All ages.

How It's Done: One partner does a breakdown on his partner and makes sure to use good skill. This drill can be done in a variety of ways, but I like to have my athletes do a specific breakdown for an allotted amount of time (usually ranging from 30 seconds to 1 minute). I prefer that both partners do his drill with 100% cooperation so the skill can be better developed. You can also do this in a set for a specific number of repetitions. For instance, you can do 10 breakdowns, then let your partner do 10 breakdowns and do 3 or 4 sets of 10 in this way. This is a great way to practice your breakdowns and develop the instinctive behavior needed to make these skills work in a real situation. Some athletes seem to have a problem doing drills where they cooperate with each other, thinking that it's not macho to be a good training partner and let your teammate work his moves on you. Remember, if all you do is fight while on the mat or in the gym, you won't ever develop your technical skill to anything other than rudimentary. It takes disciplined and directed training to be a champion.

Bryan is standing and Drew is on all fours. Bryan will drill on a Belt and Nelson Breakdown in this series of photos. Drew is being a good partner and cooperating completely with Bryan so Bryan can develop his skill in this breakdown better. If Bryan wants, Drew can offer varying degrees of resistance to make the drill more like and actual match.

Bryan moves to his side and starts his breakdown, in this case, the Belt and Nelson.

Bryan drives Drew over with the breakdown.

Bryan finishes the drill with a pin.

Here's another example of Matwork Uchikomi. Eric is doing the Spinning Cross-body Armlock on Chuck. Matwork Uchikomi can be done with any groundfighting skill (whether it's a pin, armlock, choke or leglock, or any skill for that matter) from any starting position.

Eric shrimps to his left and starts his Spinning Juji Gatame (Cross-body Armlock).

Eric rolls Chuck over and will follow through with the armlock.

Eric finishes the drill by lightly applying the armlock making sure to not injure his partner.

This photo shows the group practicing the Spinning Cross-body Armlock Drill at a typical workout.

Spin and Pin Drill (Spin and Stretch Drill)

Purpose: This drill is excellent for teaching how to follow through to the groundwork from a throw or takedown. It's also good as a transition move when your opponent is on his knees and you want to take him to the mat. I recommend doing this drill just about every practice so you can get used to finishing off your opponent with a pin or submission technique.

Age Level: All ages.

How It's Done: You start standing and your partner is on his knees. You place your right heel against the outside of his right knee and flex your knees. Use your left hand to grab his sleeve and your right hand to grab his jacket between the shoulders (not on the collar as this isn't a strong grip from this position). Spin your partner over and immediately follow him to the mat with either a pin or a submission technique. I like to have my athletes follow to the mat with a Scarf Hold or Chest Hold if they do the Spin and Pin and if they do the Spin and Stretch, follow the partner to the mat and use a Cross-body Armlock or Cross-body Leglock. Do this as a timed drill or in a set number of repetitions. I recommend that this be done with 100% cooperation from your partner, as this is a great drill that teaches a specific skill.

Bryan is standing and Trevor is on his knees.

Bryan steps across Trevor and starts his spinning takedown.

Bryan takes Trevor to the mat.

Bryan quickly follows Trevor to the mat and holds him with a Scarf Hold. This is the Spin and Pin and if Bryan wanted to do the Spin and Stretch, he could have followed Trevor to the mat and finished him with a Cross-body Armlock or Cross-body Leglock.

Here's the **Spin and Stretch variation of this drill.**

Steve spins Bill to the mat.

As Bill goes to his side, Steve starts the armlock (thus, the word "stretch" because Steve will stretch Bill's arm out).

Steve steps over Bill with his left foot and squats deep on his shoulder to roll back to apply the armlock.

Steve rolls back and stretches Bill's arm with a Cross-body Armlock.

Back and Forth Drill

Purpose: To become fluid when moving from one side to the other when doing a submission hold or technique. This is a good drill to reinforce an already-learned skill so that the person doing it can instinctively move from one position to another without losing control of his or her opponent and secure the technique.

Age Level: Teens and adults.

How It's Done: You can do this drill with any technique in groundfighting or in standing situations as well. This drill can either be timed or done in a set number of repetitions. I recommend that you do this drill with both partners cooperating 100% so that the person doing it can better learn how to control his opponent and quickly move to the other side.

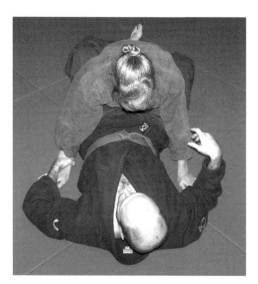

Kelly is on his back with Sharon as his partner.

Kelly rolls to his left and does a Bent Armlock.

Kelly immediately releases the armlock and rolls to his right side and does the Bent Armlock from that side.

Pin Switch Drill

Purpose: This drill teaches you to move from one pin or hold to another without losing control of your opponent. This drill also develops good skill at position and how to use your position to your advantage.

Age Level: All ages.

How It's Done: You pin your partner with any hold-down and immediately switch to another while keeping control of him the entire time. This can be done with varying degrees of cooperation, but I recommend you do it with your partner giving 100% cooperation to start so you can develop good skill moving from one pin or hold to another. You can do this drill with any technique and move from a pin to an armlock, an armlock to a pin, a pin to a leglock, an armlock to a choke, a pin to a choke or a choke to an armlock, or any combination of techniques and positions you want.

Jarrod starts out with a Chest Hold on Chris.

Jarrod shifts his position and is starting to make a switch to another pin.

Jarrod sits through and pins Chris with Rear Scarf Hold.

Jarrod moves to another pin and makes sure to keep Chris under control during his transition.

Jarrod pins Chris with a Vertical Pin and finishes the drill at this point.

Lock Ins (Also Called Pin Escape Drill)

Purpose: This drill develops strong holding and pinning skills as well as skill in escaping a pin or hold-down.

Age Level: All ages.

How It's Done: The top grappler pins his partner and the bottom grappler tries to escape. This is a tough drill and usually done with both grapplers going 100% to either hold his partner to the mat or to try to escape. This is a timed drill and I time whatever the time limit of the sport we're training for dictates (25 seconds for a judo match or 20 seconds for a sambo match).

Drew has Bryan in a Scarf Hold (Head and Arm Pin).

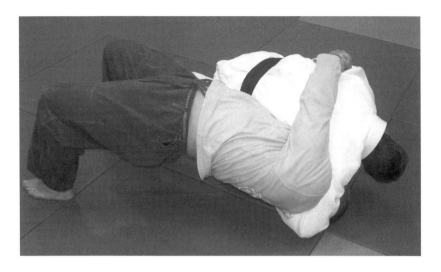

Bryan attempts to escape with both athletes going full tilt against each other.

Lock Ins (2-on-1)

Purpose: This is a tough drill and is great for a warm-up but is also useful as a way of developing mental toughness in athletes. The bottom grappler is really stuck with 2 people holding him, but it's his job to try to escape.

Age Level: All ages.

How It's Done: Two teammates hold the third athlete down with a pin and the bottom athlete tries to escape. This is a timed drill and I usually give them 25 to 30 seconds to try to escape.

In this variation of this drill, Corinna and Alan are holding Kirk to the mat in a variation of the Scarf Hold.

This variation of the drill shows Kirk controlling Corinna's upper body with an Upper Chest Hold and Alan controlling her lower body by grabbing and holding her legs.

Leg Lace Drill

Purpose: This is a great drill for developing good ankle and foot locks. I first learned this drill in sambo and this is an important drill for anyone who wants to work on their skills in leg submissions. This also develops good skill at ankle lock defense as well.

Age Level: Adults.

How To Do It: Both partners sit on their buttocks facing each other and let each other do a straight ankle lock on the partner's extended leg. At the coach's command, both athletes try to secure an ankle lock. Each athlete will also try to wrench his ankle and foot free from his partner or try to defend against his partner's ankle lock. When one partner secures the lock, the other immediately tapes out to insure safety while training. I usually run this drill for a 30 to 40 second time period.

The guys are seated facing each other and ready to start the drill. You can do the same leg, opposite legs or any variation you want.

John and Mark are working hard to secure an ankle lock on each other in this Leg Lace Drill.

Scramble Leg Lock Drill
(Also Called Leg Fishing or Leg Hunting)

Purpose: This drill teaches you to aggressively go for an ankle or leg lock.

Age Level: Adults.

How It's Done: Both partners sit on their buttocks facing each other with their knees bent and feet on the floor. At the coach's signal, they each try to secure an ankle lock and force the other to tap out. It's important to immediately tap out when you know you've been locked and immediately release pressure when your partner taps out or signals defeat in any way.

This is a fun drill that makes you appreciate your lower body and leg wrestling more than ever. If you want to develop good leglocks, especially ankle locks, and also develop a good defense against leglocks, this drill is ideal.

Guard Pass or Rollover Drill

Purpose: This drill is useful for learning how to get past your opponent's guard or if you are the grappler on the bottom, how to roll your opponent over and control him.

Age Level: All ages.

How It's Done: This is an active, competitive and aggressive drill. Both grapplers should go all out with 100% resistance. A fun way to do this drill is for one grappler to stay out and take on each teammate one at a time. The grappler who stays out is usually the bottom man. If a new grappler comes out and gets past the guard of the man who has been up, he takes his place and gets on the bottom position. It can also be done with more cooperation, or total cooperation, for athletes who are new and learning the skills of fighting from this position.

Josh is using his feet and hands to keep Travis from getting past his legs in this drill. Travis' goal is to pass Josh's guard and get a good position on him. Josh's goal is to keep Travis from doing it and rolling him over to take control.

Arm Lever Drill
(Also Called Leg Press Drill or Pry Arm Drill)

Purpose: This drill gives the top grappler an opportunity to practice his arm levers where he pries his opponent's arm free to apply the Cross-body Armlock.

Age level: Adults.

How It's Done: The top grappler has his partner in the leg press position and executes his favorite arm lever to pry the bottom man's arm free so the top grappler can apply the Cross-body Armlock. I like to have my athletes do this with total cooperation from the bottom grappler so the top athlete can develop excellent skill in this important area or groundfighting. However, we do this as a Leg Press Drill where the top athlete must hold the bottom man on the ground with the leg press position and attempt to pry the bottom man's arms free to apply the armlock. In this case, the bottom grappler offers varying degrees of resistance up to doing his best o keep his arm from being pried free and locked. If you want to get good at the Cross-body Armlock and controlling the position and prying an opponent's arm free, this drill is one you should do a lot. I have the athletes to a set of 10 repetitions on each arm of his partner, then let the bottom man have his turn.

In this photo, I have Bill in the leg press position and am starting to work the lever to pry his arm free.

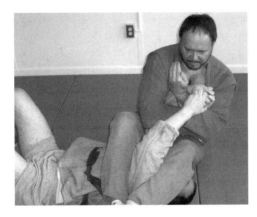

I'm prying his arm free at this point.

The drill is completed and I've pried his arm free. Bill can offer 100% cooperation or 100% resistance, depending on what we want to do.

Rodeo Ride Drill

Purpose: This drill develops the vital skill of sinking your hooks (legs) in and controlling your opponent with effective leg control.

Age Level: All ages.

How to Do It: This drill can be done with 100% cooperation or 100% resistance. One athlete will get his partner in a rodeo ride and roll him around the mat, flatten him out and control him as much as possible. This drill can be done in carrying degrees of cooperation and I usually time this drill allowing each grappler 30 seconds to 1 minute. It's a good idea to start out with both grapplers cooperating 100% so the skill of doing the rodeo ride can be learned and appreciated.

Steve is controlling Bret with a rodeo ride. Steve makes sure to dig his legs and feet in and control Bret's upper body at the lapels.

Steve rolls Bret around the mat controlling him the entire time. The rodeo ride is an important skill and is used to set up and opponent for many pins and submission techniques.

Don't Let Him Up Drill
(also called Pin the Guard Drill)

Purpose: This is a fitness drill as much as a skill drill but the idea is for the top grappler to be between his partner's legs and not let him get up. This drill is really for the bottom grappler who has his opponent in his guard and wants to get up, roll him over, sweep him or get away. This drill teaches the bottom man that he needs to keep constant pressure on his opponent; especially from the guard and that the guard is not always where you want to hang out in a fight. It also teaches the top grappler good position, because if you can pin somebody from their guard, you can almost certainly stick them from side control or mount. This is a very physical drill and great for fitness training as well.

Age Level: All ages.

How It's Done: The bottom man has his partner in his guard and the top grappler tries to hold the bottom athlete to the mat any way he can. He doesn't try any submission, but only wants to keep his partner from getting up. The bottom grappler tries to get up off his back and on to his feet. He doesn't try any submissions or rollovers either, but only wants to be up off his back and escape his partner's hold. This drill should be timed for 30 to 60 seconds allowing the grapplers time to work.

Nick has Alan held to the mat and Alan is trying to get up. If Alan gets up, he's successful. This is a good drill that I've used for a long time and is also a favorite drill of Jarrod Fobes at his grappling club.

Guard Pin Drill
(Sambo Chest Hold Drill)

Purpose: This drill is good for sambo because this is a hold-down that can earn you points. The purpose of this drill is for the top grappler to keep his partner from getting up and teaches him to control the bottom man. This is similar to the Lock-In drill and a very physical drill that emphasizes fitness development.

Age Level: Adults and older teens.

How It's Done: The athletes get into a closed guard position. The top grappler's job is to keep his partner from getting off his back and escaping. The bottom man must do everything he can to get up off his back. The top grappler's job is to stick his partner to the mat and keep the space between them to a minimum. The top grappler doesn't want to pass the bottom man's guard or do anything other than keep the bottom grappler flat on his back. The bottom grappler's job is to try to get up, roll the top man over (sweep him), or try a submission technique to escape this bad position. Both grapplers usually go with total resistance, but this drill can be done with varying degrees of cooperation if the goal is to teach skills on what to do from this situation.

Chris is holding Alan to the mat on his back. Alan must do everything he can to escape from the bottom position.

Wrestler's Ride Drill

Purpose: This drill teaches good control and position using the wrestler's ride. Riding an opponent is an important skill in groundfighting and this drill teaches it well.

Age Level: All ages.

How It's Done: The top grappler rides his partner with a wrestler's ride and continually tries to control him and keep him on all fours or flat on his front. The bottom man can offer varying degrees of resistance. I like to time this drill with the athletes going about 30 seconds.

Erik is riding Nick with a wrestler's ride. This is a good drill and teaches the top grappler how to control his opponent and set him up for a breakdown.

Get Up Drill

Purpose: This drill teaches the athlete who is standing how to keep his opponent from getting to his feet and teaches the bottom grappler (on his knees) how to get up from the mat to engage his opponent. This is an aggressive drill and not for the recreational or novice athlete.

Age Level: Adults and teens.

How It's Done: The top grappler stands in front of his partner who is on his knees or on all fours. The bottom grappler must try to get up and the top grappler must try to keep him from getting up. This drill also teaches mental toughness and is physically demanding. I do this as a timed drill usually allowing 30 seconds per round. This can also be done with each grappler changing positions when the bottom man is able to stand up.

The top grapplers in this drill training session are doing their best to keep the bottom grappler from getting up.

Spinning Drill

Purpose: This drill develops good balance and movement and allows the athletes to appreciate the importance of being in a good position while groundfighting. It's also a great fitness drill.

Age Level: All ages.

How It's Done: there are 2 ways that I like. One is spinning around your partner's body using your hands and the other is spinning around him without using your hands. You spin around your partner and when the coach says "switch" you change directions and spin the opposite direction. The coach will say, "switch" several times during the 30 to 40 seconds the drill lasts.

Here's the start of the drill. Bryan has his chest flat on Drew's back.

Bryan spins around Drew and when the coach says, "switch" he changes direction and spins the opposite direction.

Here's the no hands variation of this drill. This teaches good body contact and distribution of weight.

Snap Down and Go Behind Drill

Purpose: This drill teaches the top grappler to quickly get behind his opponent and control him with a wrestler's ride (or any ride for that matter, such as the rodeo ride or any control position).

Age Level: All ages.

How It's Done: One athlete is standing and the other is on his knees or all fours. The standing athlete will snap his partner down to the mat and quickly get behind him and get a wrestler's ride.

Bryan is standing with Trevor on his knees.

Bryan snaps Trevor down to the mat making sure to control him with his hands and arms.

Bryan quickly moves behind Trevor and establishes a ride.

Mat Chess

Purpose: This is an advanced drill for grapplers who like to explore new ways to try groundfighting and think as they go.

Age Level: Adults.

How It's Done: This is an action-reaction-action drill that teaches position where the partners take turns. When it's your turn, your partner can only stay in the position that he ended his last turn in; he can't alter anything to resist you. One grappler chooses the starting position and the other grappler gets the first turn. Gaining position, transitioning, attempting an escape or a submission all count as one turn. This drill makes you think and you have to make makes up what you will do based on what your partner does similar to a chess game. The goal is to react to your partner's position as quickly as possible and move into that position. Be sure to tell your partner the move you will do, and then do it. If you get good at this drill, it can be a fairly fast paced drill. You can go as many moves as you and your partner want. I've seen several variations of this drill, but this one by Jarrod Fobes is my favorite.

Jarrod has chosen to be in Chris' guard as his starting position. Be sure to tell your partner what position you will do, and then do it. He cooperates with you, and then it's his job to tell you what position he will do to react to your initial position.

Chris tells Jarrod he is going to shrimp to his side and then does it.

Jarrod tells Chris he will stack him and then does it.

Chris Tells Jarrod he will do a spinning cross-body armlock and then does it.

Jarrod tells Chris he'll stack him on his shoulders to counter the armlock, then does it.

Chris tells Jarrod he's going out the back door with the Cross-body Armlock and then does it. Chris and Jarrod decided to end their mat chess game at this point.

Flat Drill

Purpose: This drill teaches how to control the position and ride your opponent. In the first way to do it and in the second way to do it, it teaches you how to work out of this situation.

Age Level: All ages.

How It's Done: There are 2 ways to do this drill: one is for the top grappler and one is for the bottom grappler. The first way is to have the top grappler get his hooks in his partner and flatten him out with a rodeo ride. His job is to keep his partner flat on his front and control him in this ride for as long as the coach times the drill. The second way to do this drill is for the bottom grappler who is flat on his face attempt to get up and escape this situation. The coach times this drill for 30 to 40 seconds. Go several rounds.

The team is working on the Flat Drill. This teaches how to control your opponent with a rodeo ride and keep him flat on his front and a vulnerable position for a choke, pin or armlock.

Make Ugly Drill

Purpose: This is a tough, physically demanding drill that tests the limits of anyone who does it. It makes you rough, tough and aggressive and pushes your aerobic fitness to its limits. Make sure you have the puke bucket ready.

Age Level: Adults. This drill isn't for children!

How It's Done: This is for advanced and elite athletes and not for recreational athletes or children. The group makes a circle and one grappler is in the middle kneeling on both knees. The first opponent comes into the circle and is standing. The grappler on his knees must try to get up and throw his opponent. The opponent's job is to keep snapping the grappler in the middle down to the mat and not let him get to his feet. After 20 to 30 seconds (the coach is timing each round or match), a new, fresh opponent replaces the other. The grappler who started on his knees must stay in the circle until he has fought everyone in the circle, one by one. The new, fresh opponent is allowed to immediately pounce on the grappler on his knees and not let him up. Eventually, the poor guy in the middle will fade physically and pretty much get pulled around. He'll try to fight as hard as possible, but it's tough to do. I first did this drill when I was training with Rene Pommerelle and was totally wasted when the 7 people in the circle were through with me. As a coach, I use this drill sparingly and as a way of making my athletes more aggressive. It's a real fighting and survival drill and I'm not kidding when I say have the puke bucket ready.

Bryan is on his knees trying to get up as Trevor snaps him back down to the mat and won't let him up. Bryan's goal is to get up and throw Trevor, but it's extremely hard to do when the top man is yanking you around and slamming you back down to the mat. This drill isn't for the faint of heart or for anyone that isn't in top shape or unwilling or able to take the rough action.

Linking Drill or Flow Drill

Purpose: This drill teaches you to move from one position or technique to another as smoothly as possible and teaches combination techniques in groundfighting. It can also be used in standing situations as well. It takes total cooperation on the part of both athletes.

Age level: Adults and older teens.

How It's Done: One athlete will start the drill by breaking his partner down and applying a specific hold or submission technique. His partner cooperates 100% and allows the first grappler to move from the initial skill to another, then another, then even another. The goal is to link as many moves together as possible. It's important to keep this drill as realistic as possible and this teaches you to move from one stable position to another, all the while keeping control of your partner or opponent.

Jake starts the drill with a Spinning Cross-body Armlock on Josh.

Jake rolls Josh over and maintains control.

Jake moves into a Straddle Pin.

Josh offers some resistance and Jake starts to change to another move.

Jake finishes the drill is a Cross-body Armlock. This drill teaches you how to use combinations and move from one technique to another without losing control of your opponent.

Crash Pad Throwing Drills

Purpose: Throwing on the crash pad develops throws with full force and effect. I recommend training on the crash pads every practice if you are in a sport or martial art that includes throwing. Crash pads are a great addition to any training room and provide additional safety in throwing practice.

Age Level: Older kids, teens and adults.

How It's Done: We usually do this drill by having several guys in line at the end of the pad and each takes turns throwing everyone in line. Try to take the time so that everyone can get in at least 50 throws in each practice if possible. You can also do this for time. You can vary this drill so that each person does as many throws as possible in 1 minute. This is a tough drill and you've never thought one minute could be so long. Don't laugh at doing this until you try it. It's important to remember that taking falls on the crash pad isn't a substitute for learning and doing good breakfalls. Breakfalls are an important form of safety in throwing practice and should be mastered to insure your protection and avoid injury.

Kelly is throwing Nikolay during crash pad drills. The extra protection of a thick foam crash pad allows you to throw your partners with full force and control. I recommend that every club or training facility have at least one crash pad to insure safer and more effective training for throws and takedowns.

Uchikomi and Throwing on the Crash Pad

Purpose: This is a good skill drill that combines uchikomi (fitting practice) with a full throw on the pad with power. It gives you a chance to experience the feel of fitting in as perfectly as possible on the uchikomi followed immediately by a throw done at full speed and power. This is a very good drill for advanced and elite athletes to get a better "feel" for their throwing techniques.

Age Level: Adults and older teens.

How It's Done: At the edge of a crash pad, you do a single uchikomi on your partner and make it as "perfect" as you can. As soon as you come out of your uchikomi, immediately fit in again and throw your partner with full power onto the crash pad. You and your partner can take turns.

Bryan does a single uchikomi, then immediately throws Nikolay.

This drill teaches how to perfect and personalize a throw to suit your body.

I Throw, You Throw (Trade Throws)

Purpose: This is a great timing drill that develops a high level of skill for throwing.

Age Level: All ages.

How It's Done: This isn't a crash pad drill, so use the mat or tatami. It's an active, moving drill that improves your timing in throwing techniques. You and your partner can do this drill standing still on the mat or moving about the mat and trade throws. This is one of the oldest drills in judo, but is a great drill to develop timing in your throws and I recommend you do this while moving. But before you do this in a moving fashion, I recommend that beginners do this drill in a static manner so the technique can be better developed. However, in reality, most throws are done against a moving opponent, so this is a good drill to develop the movement, gripping, posture and tempo skills necessary to have effective throwing skills. Take turns throwing each other for a specific period of time or for a set number of repetitions. You and your partner can work on a specific throw or mix them up, depending on what you want to do. This is done with full cooperation usually, but can be done with a slight amount of resistance, however I believe you get more benefit from the drill if you cooperate fully with each other.

Roy is throwing Bryan and as soon as he gets up off the mat, Bryan will throw Roy.

You Never Know When I'll Say Throw Drill

Purpose: This drill teaches athletes to react quickly and throw on the signal of the coach. This is an Uchikomi and Throw Drill. The athletes never know when the coach will tell them to throw their partners.

Age Level: Best for kids, but adults can do this as well.

How It's Done: Your partner stands still (this isn't usually a moving drill, but it can be) and you will do uchikomi (repetition fit-ins) on your coach's count. The coach will yell, "Throw" at any time during the uchikomi count. He could say 1…2…3…Throw with you doing an uchikomi each time, then throwing on his signal. You never know when the coach will tell you to throw. This uneven cadence or count forces you to be ready to throw at any time and not get complacent in doing your uchikomi training. I usually don't have a count of more than 10 at any time. I usually have the athletes use their favorite throw for this drill. Go several rounds of this with each athlete.

Kirk is fitting in with his favorite throw on Corinna waiting for the coach to yell, "throw."

125

Walk and Throw on Crash Pad

Purpose: This drill develops confidence in the fitting in phase of your throws. This drill reinforces good habits of body control that are necessary for good skill in throwing.

Age Level: All ages.

How It's Done: On one end of the mat, fit in for your favorite throw and pick your partner up. When you load him up using good form, walk him to the other side of the mat where you have a crash pad. As soon as you get to the crash pad, throw your partner. Take turns for a specific period of time or a set number of repetitions.

Bryan fits in on Nikolay with a Shoulder Throw.

Bryan has Nikolay loaded up and starts to walk toward the crash pad. It's important for Bryan to maintain good balance and keep good throwing form the entire time.

Bryan takes Nikolay to the crash pad and immediately throws him onto the pad.

Uchikomi Training

Purpose: Uchikomi develops timing, skill in throwing or groundfighting, foot speed, footwork and all aspects of skill in throwing or groundfighting situations. The word "uchikomi" is translated to mean "repetitive fitting practice." The uchikomi discussed here deals with standing or throwing uchikomi. I equate uchikomi training to the shadow boxing that boxers do. It's a great way to develop your throwing skills without having to take a lot of falls and it's one of the best ways I know to develop foot speed and a fluid movement that is vital to being good at the skills of throwing. One of the hardest parts of throwing an opponent is the middle part of the movement, what the Japanese call "tsukuri" or the building (fitting in) phase of the throw. Uchikomi training can develop your skills in all phases of throwing, but especially in this hard-to-learn "fitting in" phase of the throw. It doesn't matter what you call it, and whether you're doing judo, sambo, jujitsu, submission grappling or wrestling, uchikomi should be part of your drill training routine to improve your throwing skills.

Age Level: All ages.

How It's Done: Uchikomi can be done stationary (static) or moving in any direction. Uchikomi is a movement repeated over and over again so that it becomes instinctive. There are many ways to do uchikomi training and one of the biggest misconceptions people have is that uchikomi is only done for throwing and standing. Doing a skill or technique repeatedly for a breakdown or groundwork set up is just as much of an uchikomi as doing it for a throw. But I'm discussing uchikomi for throwing right now and there are many different Uchikomi drills you can use. Here are some examples:

1. Do in Sets: I do a set of 10 uchikomi and you do a set of 10. We repeat this for a pre-determined amount of sets (for instance, we do 5 sets of 10). You can do this standing or while moving about the mat.

2. I Hit, You Hit: I'll do an uchikomi and you immediately follow with your own immediately after I finish. We can do this for a set number of repetitions or with a partner or coach timing us.

3. Uchikomi and Throw: I fit in for an uchikomi, come out and hit back in immediately with a throw. An example is I'll do an uchikomi for a Shoulder throw, then immediately come in a second time and actually throw my partner with the Shoulder Throw.

4. Directional Uchikomi: I'll move backward with my partner following me and do my uchikomi down the length of the mat. He'll do the same thing going the other way. Another example is that I'll move sideways down the length of the mat and do uchikomi. My partner will do the same going back.

5. Four-Way Uchikomi: This is a variation of the Directional Uchikomi. I move to my left and do a Shoulder throw uchikomi, then I'll move to my right and do the same thing, then I'll move forward and do a Shoulder Throw uchikomi, then I'll move backward and do the same thing. I go in all four directions doing the same throw. My partner will do the same thing, working on the throw he wants to do. Each time I do this, it's a "set" and I'll do 10 sets as will my partner.

Kirk is doing uchikomi for a forward throw on Corinna in this photo.

Gym Floor Uchikomi

Purpose: This drill allows the athletes to develop better control of their uchikomi skills and develops better control in the actual fit-in phase of the throw. Also, this drill allows the athletes to do more uchikomi that normally done because of the constraints of the mat size.

Age Level: Teens and adults.

How It's Done: This can be done in a gym, outside on the grass, a track or any flat surface. The athletes can wear shoes if they wish, but when I have my athletes do this in the gym, they go barefoot to help toughen the feet. This is a moving drill and has the athletes move in lines, angles or randomly about the gym. John Saylor used to have his judo athletes at the U.S. Olympic Training Center run up hills in the Cheyenne Mountains near Colorado Springs, Colorado and do uchikomi at the flat spot at the top of the steep mountain pass they ran.

Nikolay and Chris are doing gym uchikomi. This drill teaches good control of every phase of the attack. Make sure you don't accidentally throw your opponent!

Grip Randori
(also called Grip Fencing or Jacket Pummeling)

Purpose: To teach aggressive gripping skills and an aggressive attitude in going for the dominant grip.

Age Level: All ages.

How It's Done: This is a practice match with grip fighting only. No throws or takedowns are allowed, just hard, aggressive grip fighting. This drill is great for teaching how to control an opponent with your grip. It's a good idea to have the grip in mind you want to use for your favorite and most effective throw and try to dominate your training partners with it. This is an essential drill for anyone who wants to excel and judo, sambo or other sports where grip fighting is so important. If you are in a "no gi" sport, you can do this drill without the jacket. I usually time this drill for 30 to 40 seconds and the athletes go full blast. This is a very competitive drill and helps develop an aggressive attitude as well.

Drew and Bryan are fighting hard to dominate the grip in this drill. Remember, this is a practice match without the throws or takedowns; gripping only.

Push Pull Drill

Purpose: In grip fighting, things can change quickly. This drill emphasizes the quick action needed when gripping. You never know when you'll have to push or pull your opponent. This develops strength as well and is a good fitness drill.

Age Level: Adults and teens.

How It's Done: The athletes stand and take a neutral grip. On the coach's signal of "push," they push on each other until the coach yells "pull" and they immediately have to pull on each other. The athletes never know when the coach will yell "push" or "pull" and the coach should vary the times that he does yell commands. I run this drill for about 30-second rounds and let the guys switch to a new partner as soon as each round is completed.

Drew and Bryan are pushing on each other.

At the coach's signal, Drew and Bryan immediately pull on each other.

Pulling Drill

Purpose: This drill develops a strong grip and is a good strength drill.

Age Level: All ages.

How It's Done: This drill can be done several ways. The first way is for both athletes to lay flat on their fronts with their knees bent and ankles crossed. The second way is for the athletes to sit on their buttocks and pull. The third way is for the athletes to kneel on both knees and pull. The fourth way is for the athletes to stand and pull on each other. This forces them to use only their upper bodies. Each grappler pulls as hard as possible and tries to pull his partner toward him. They well both scoot backwards in an attempt to pull their partner to them. I usually time this drill for 30 seconds.

Rob and Kevin are laying flat on their fronts pulling on each other in this drill that emphasizes grip strength and upper body strength. This variation of the drill is great for kids and I've used it often.

This photo shows Rob and Kevin sitting on their buttocks pulling on each other.

This drill can be done with the athletes both kneeling as shown.

The standing version of this drill is shown here. It's important that the athletes try to maintain a good posture when pulling and not get into the bad habit of bending over.

Situational Grip Fighting

Purpose: To teach how to dominate the grip as well as how to counter a dominant grip.

Age Level: All ages.

How It's Done: One athlete will get his best grip on his partner. The partner's job is to try to break the grip and counter with his own and end up in a dominant position. This is useful if you know that an opponent does a specific grip and you want to work on countering it or fighting it off. You can do this in varying degrees of resistance from total cooperation to total resistance. I usually have the athletes do this in 20 to 30 second rounds.

Bryan has Drew in a strong back grip and Drew's job is to fight out of it and try to gain a better grip for himself.

Movement Drills

Purpose: These drills teach athletes how to move freely and gracefully with good posture, balance, footwork and coordination. Good movement is vital to being able to perform throwing and takedown skills on any level.

Age Level: All ages, but especially for kids and novices.

How To Do It: There are a variety of ways of doing this drill. A good way I like to have my athletes drill is to move with each other sideways. The idea is for the athletes to move gracefully, never crossing their feet (crossing your feet is asking to have an opponent foot sweep you). Learning how to move in different directions with good posture and always in being in position to attack or defend if vital to any grappler. Moving about the mat randomly with your partner is a good drill as well. Once you have a good ability at moving with each other as a team, step it up a bit and offer resistance to each other. One athlete will try to dominate the other and control how he moves. Remember to always keep good posture and be in position to attack and defend.

This drill teaches the athletes how to move to the side with good posture and tempo. Knowing how to move around the mat is important if you want to be able to throw people around the mat.

Knockdown Drill
(also called Winner Stays Up or Takedown Drill)

Purpose: This drill teaches aggressive grappling and is a great fighting drill.

Age Level: Older kids, teens and adults.

How It's Done: A grappler takes on the line. Each grappler attempts to throw or take his opponent down to the mat. One athlete wins if his opponent touches anything other than the bottom of his feet. If a grappler is knocked down to his knee or knees, falls to his buttocks or is taken off his feet in any way, he has to sit down and the winner stays up to fight another opponent. You can do this with groundfighting as well with the winner who stays out starting in the guard position and the challenger starts on his knees between his partner's legs. The winner is the one who passes the guard or rolls his opponent over (sweeps his opponent). I usually have the matches last no longer than 1 minute or so. If there is a draw, both athletes sit down and 2 new athletes take their place.

Bryan took Drew down to the mat in this photo. The loser in this drill is the athlete who touches the mat with anything other than the bottom of his feet. It's a competitive drill and emphasizes aggressive grappling.

Toe Tap Game

Purpose: This drill is great for teaching how to move your feet and foot sweep an opponent. It's also a good drill to teach timing and quick foot movement, especially for kids.

Age Level: All ages, but especially an especially good drill for kids.

How It's Done: Each partner holds his lapels or places his hands behind his back so he won't use his hands at all. One athlete is the attacker and the other is the defender. The attacker attempts to "tap" the top of the defender's foot with his foot. Use either foot and try to tap (don't stomp) the defender's feet as pOssible in 30 seconds. The defender's job is to avoid getting either of his feet tapped and can move freely to avoid getting them tapped. The only rule is that the defender cannot move directly backward or turn his back to the attacker. This is a fun drill that teaches good foot speed and aggressively going for a foot sweep.

Bryan and Drew are ready to start the drill. They stand about 2 feet apart.

Bryan is the attacker this time and is trying to "tap" the top of Drew's feet. You can use either foot and move freely about the mat. This is an active skill drill and good for some cardio work as well.

Randori
(Free Practice, Practice Matches, Going Live, Rolling)

Purpose: Randori is a mainstay of training. Whether you call it randori, going live, free grappling, rolling, practice matches or any other name, it's one of the best ways there is to develop good fighting and grappling skills.

Age Level: All ages.

How It's Done: First and foremost; randori is training, not an actual match. You will take plenty of falls and get tapped out plenty of times and do the same to your training partners as well! You can do various levels of randori, but Bryan Potter came up with the phrase "smiling randori" to describe a light, training and developmental approach to this type of training. If you can smile during randori, then you're not going full tilt and this is usually about 50% effort. This is a good level for novices or if you're not in the mood to go full blast with your training partners. Randori is to grapplers what a sparring session is for a boxer. It's a fight, but it's a practice fight. Randori should be a learning experience and not simply a fight for survival. I believe that if you start standing in randori, you should always follow to the mat for groundfighting after a throw. Some coaches prefer to not have their athletes engage in groundfighting after a throw in randori, but I believe that in a real match, you would immediately go to the mat and try to secure a pin or submission technique. It only makes sense to me to do the same in your workouts and randori sessions. However, if the coach believes his athletes need work on their throwing skills, he can alter the randori drill to have only throws and takedowns to meet the needs of his athletes. Also, groundfighting randori is an excellent training drill and really develops great cardio capacity as well, so make the randori fit the needs of you and your team. Your training session shouldn't consist of only going live or randori. It's good to have workouts once in a while of nothing but a warm up and lots of randori, but doing it on a regular basis just makes you tougher, not necessarily better. There are lots of tough guys, but fewer champions and using randori along with a structured training program of drill training will go a lot farther in making you a champion.

John and Will have squared off and are ready to randori.

Groundfighting Randori
(also called Newaza Randori)

Purpose: This is a drill where the athletes randori or go live in groundfighting. It's very useful for developing fighting skill, a high degree of fitness training and gives the athletes a chance to try their moves out in a competitive way during training.

Age Level: All ages.

How It's Done: Everyone pairs up and grapples on the ground. You can go varying degrees of intensity from "smiling randori" (about 50% effort and named so by Bryan Potter because it's at a level where you can smile while you're working out and not extremely hard) to going full blast. Remember, however, this is training and not an actual match. It's practice and the guys you're going with are your teammates. Make sure you take care of each other and no one gets hurt or beat up real bad. You can start in any positron you wish, but I usually have the guys start out with one sitting on his buttocks and the other kneeling in front of him.

Here's groundfighting randori at Welcome Mat. A coach supervises all randori sessions and sportsmanship and an attitude of mutual development are part of what is expected. If you want to be a champion, you have to train both hard and smart.

Drew is on his buttocks and Chas is on his knees getting ready to start their workout in groundfighting randori. You can start from any position you wish, and should change your starting positions to offer a variety of situations in training.

Jacket Randori
(Fight Your Gi Drill)

Purpose: This is a good warm up or cool down is an active, fun drill.

Age Level: Kids, but adults like this also.

How It's Done: Take off your jacket and hold it like you would if someone were wearing it. Move around the mat, throwing it with any throw you want. Kids really like this drill and I use it as a good cool down after a workout. It helps them let off a lot of steam and, as I tell my athletes, this drill helps sweep the dust off my mats!

Derrick is gripping his jacket like he would an opponent to start this drill.

Derrick throws his jacket and moves around the mat as if he were actually fighting an opponent. This is a fun drill and gives the athletes a good workout as well.

About The Author

Steve Scott holds advanced black belt rank in both Kodokan Judo and Shingitai Jujitsu and is a member of the U.S. Sombo Association's Hall of Fame. He first stepped onto a mat in 1965 as a 12-year-old boy and has been training, competing and coaching since that time. He is the head coach and founder of the Welcome Mat Judo, Jujitsu and Sambo Club in Kansas City, Missouri where he has coached hundreds of national and international champions and medal winners in judo, sambo, sport jujitsu and submission grappling. Steve served as a national coach for USA Judo, Inc., the national governing body for the sport of judo as well as the U.S. Sombo Association and the Amateur Athletic Union in the sport of sambo. He also served as the coach education program director for many years with USA Judo, Inc. He has personally coached 3 World Sambo Champions, several Pan American Games Champions and a member of the U.S. Olympic Team as well as 60 U.S. National Sambo Champions and over 150 U.S. National Judo Champions. He served as the national team coach and director of development for the under-21 national judo team and coached U.S. teams at several World Championships in both judo and sambo. He was the U.S. women's team head coach for the 1983 Pan American Games in Caracas, Venezuela where his team won 4 golds and 6 silvers and the team championship. He also coached numerous U.S. teams at many international judo and sambo events. Steve conducted numerous national training camps in judo at the U.S. Olympic Training Centers in Colorado Springs, Colorado, Marquette, Michigan and Lakes Placid, New York. He also serves as a television commentator for a local MMA production and conducts submission grappling clinics for MMA fighters. As an athlete, he competed in judo and sambo, winning 2 gold medals and a bronze medal in the National AAU Sambo Championships, as well as several other medals in smaller national sambo events and has won numerous state and regional medals in that sport. He was a state and regional champion in judo and competed in numerous national championships as well. He has trained, competed and coached in North America, South America, Europe and Japan and has the opportunity to train with some of the top judo and sambo athletes and coaches in the world.

Steve is active in the Shingitai Jujitsu Association with his friend John Saylor (www.JohnSaylor-SJA.com) and has a strong Shingitai program at his Welcome Mat Judo, Jujitsu and Sambo Club. He has authored several other books published by Turtle Press including ARMLOCK

ENCYCLOPEDIA, THE GRAPPLER'S BOOK OF STRANGLES AND CHOKES, VITAL LEGLOCKS, GROUNDFIGHTING PINS AND BREAKDOWNS and CHAMPIONSHIP SAMBO, as well as the DVD, CHAMPIONSHIP SAMBO. He has also authored COACHING ON THE MAT, SECRETS OF THE CROSS-BODY ARMLOCK (along with Bill West), THE JUJI GATAME HANDBOOK (along with Bill West), PRINCIPLES OF SHINGITAI JUJITSU (along with John Saylor) and THE MARTIAL ARTS TERMINOLOGY HANDBOOK, as well as the DVD, SECRETS OF THE CROSS-BODY ARMLOCK. Steve is also active in training law enforcement professionals with Law Enforcement and Security Trainers, Inc. (www.lesttrainers.com).

Steve is a graduate of the University of Missouri-Kansas City and teaches jujitsu, judo and sambo full-time as well as CPR and First-aid. For over thirty years, he worked as a community center director and coached judo, jujitsu and sambo in various community centers in the Kansas City area. He has conducted about 300 clinics and seminars across the United States and can be reached by e-mailing him at stevescottjudo@yahoo.com or going to www.WelcomeMatJudoClub.com. For many years, he was active as an athlete in the sport of Scottish Highland Games and was a national master's champion in that sport. He is married to Becky Scott, the first American woman to win a World Sambo Championship. Naturally, they met at a judo tournament in 1973 and have been together ever since.

Index